Carolina's Story

Sea Turtles Get Sick Too!

By Donna Rathmell
Photography by Barbara J. Bergwerf

This book is dedicated to the many people who devote hours of time caring for sea turtles and their nests. A special thanks to the staff and volunteers of the South Carolina Department of Natural Resources Turtle Rescue Team and the Sea Turtle Hospital at the South Carolina Aquarium for all their efforts on behalf of injured and sick sea turtles.

For information on the Sea Turtle Hospital at the South Carolina Aquarium and other sea turtle rehabilitative programs, go to "Carolina's Story" links at www.SylvanDellPublishing.com. All of these wonderful programs and caring people could use your support! The author and photographer donate a portion of their royalties to the Sea Turtle Hospital.

Library of Congress Control Number: 2005921088
A catalog record for this book is available from the Library of Congress.

Summary: The photo journal of "Carolina," a critically ill loggerhead sea turtle, as she is cared for and nursed back to health at the Sea Turtle Hospital. Just like hospitalized children, Carolina goes through a variety of emotions and procedures during her care, recovery process, and her eventual release back to her home - the ocean.

ISBN: 0-9764943-0-2

Loggerhead Sea Turtles-Juvenile Literature
Wildlife Rehabilitation-Juvenile Literature
Hospitalized Children-Juvenile Literature

Photograph Copyrights © Barbara Bergwerf 2005
Text and Craft Illustration Copyrights © Sylvan Dell Publishing 2005
Craft Illustrations by Matthew Ward
Text Layout and Design by Lisa Downey, studiodowney
Printed in China

Sylvan Dell Publishing
976 Houston Northcutt Blvd., Suite 3
Mt. Pleasant, SC 29464

A sea turtle had been washed up on the beach. She was barely alive and really needed help from the Turtle Rescue Team.

They took her by truck to the Sea Turtle Hospital where a team of people were waiting for her.

They named the turtle Carolina.

Dr. Tom took blood samples to see what was making Carolina so sick. He looked in her mouth - "Say ahhh." She had life-threatening "turtle flu" and was lucky she was getting the help she would need.

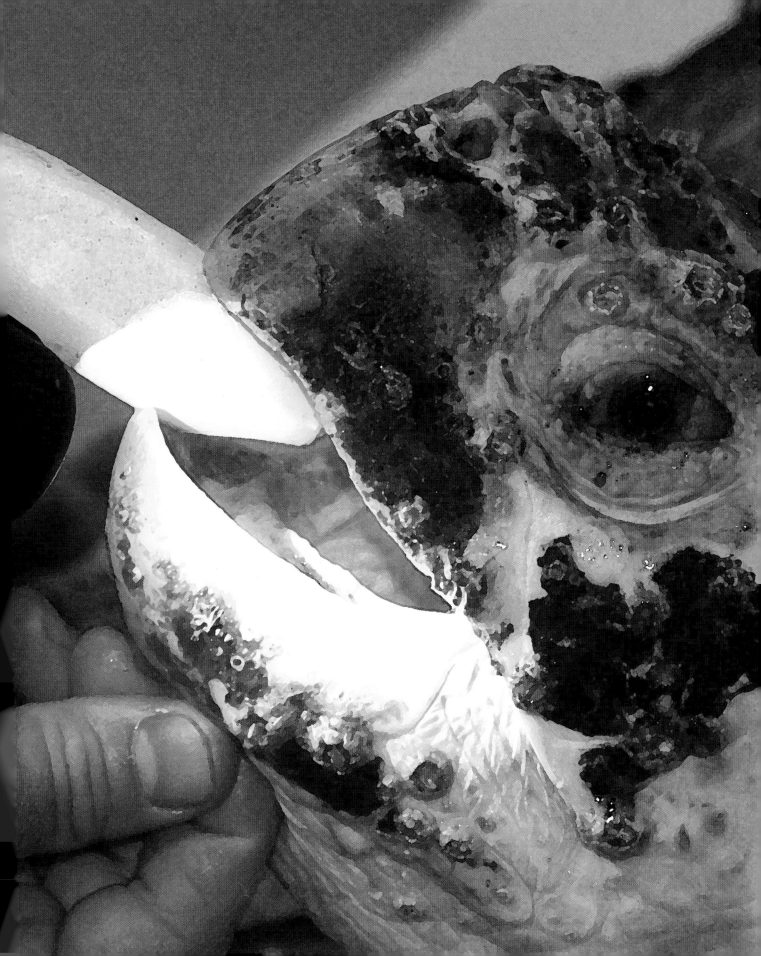

Biologist Kelly gave Carolina a shower with a hose. The shower cleaned her shell (carapace) and helped to get her blood flowing.

Carolina did not feel well and just wanted to be left alone. She even felt too sick to try to crawl away.

The next day volunteers spent hours cleaning barnacles off Carolina's shell.

Carolina did not like the feel of the brushing and scraping.

Then they rubbed antibiotic into her open sores.

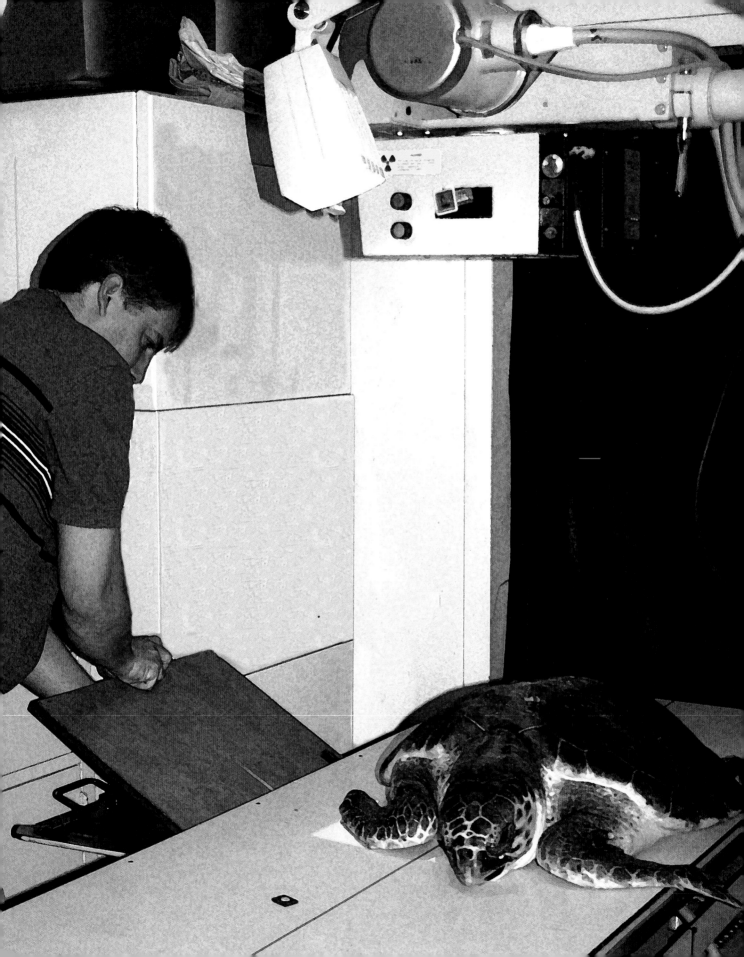

Dr. Tom took some x-rays. Poor Carolina felt so sick she did not care what they were doing to her!

If she were able to cry, Carolina would have cried and cried.

Turtles get shots too! Carolina did not like getting the shots but they did help to make her feel better.

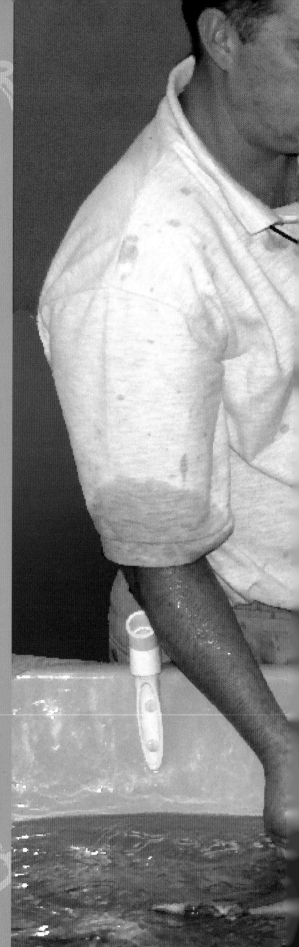

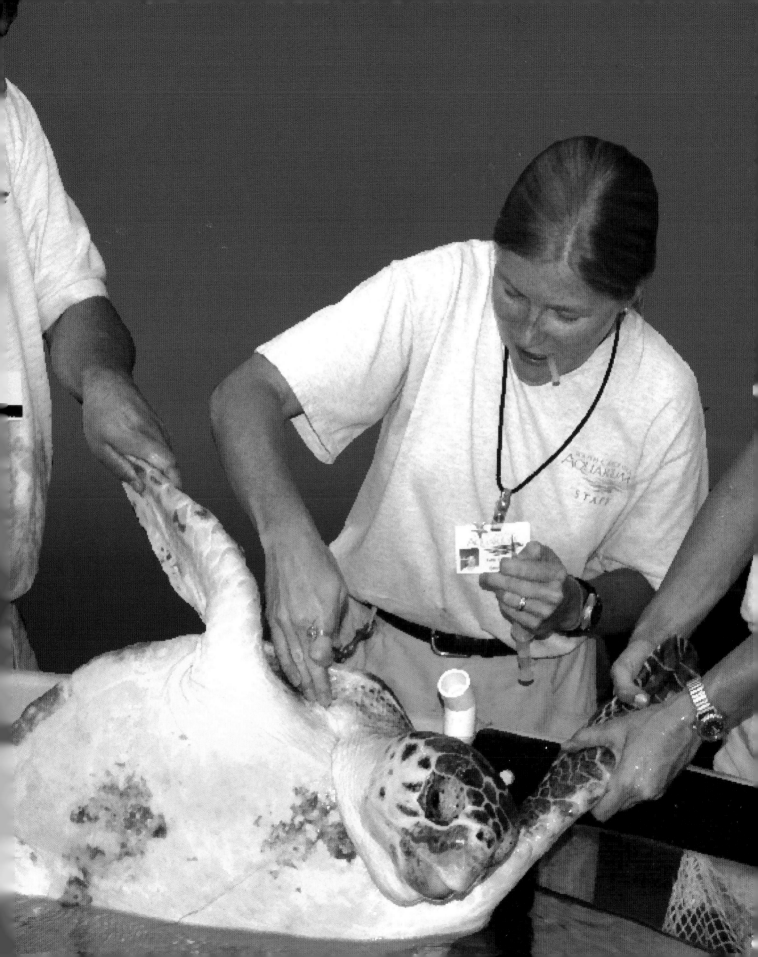

Soon Carolina was hungry. She learned that a silver-looking bowl meant food was coming. When she saw a volunteer with a bowl, she would eagerly swim over to get her dinner!

As long as Carolina was feeling so sick, she did not seem to mind her doctor exams - mostly because she did not have the energy to fight. When she started to feel better though, she did not want to get out of her tank. If she saw people coming to get her, she would try to swim away.

And then she learned to splash...

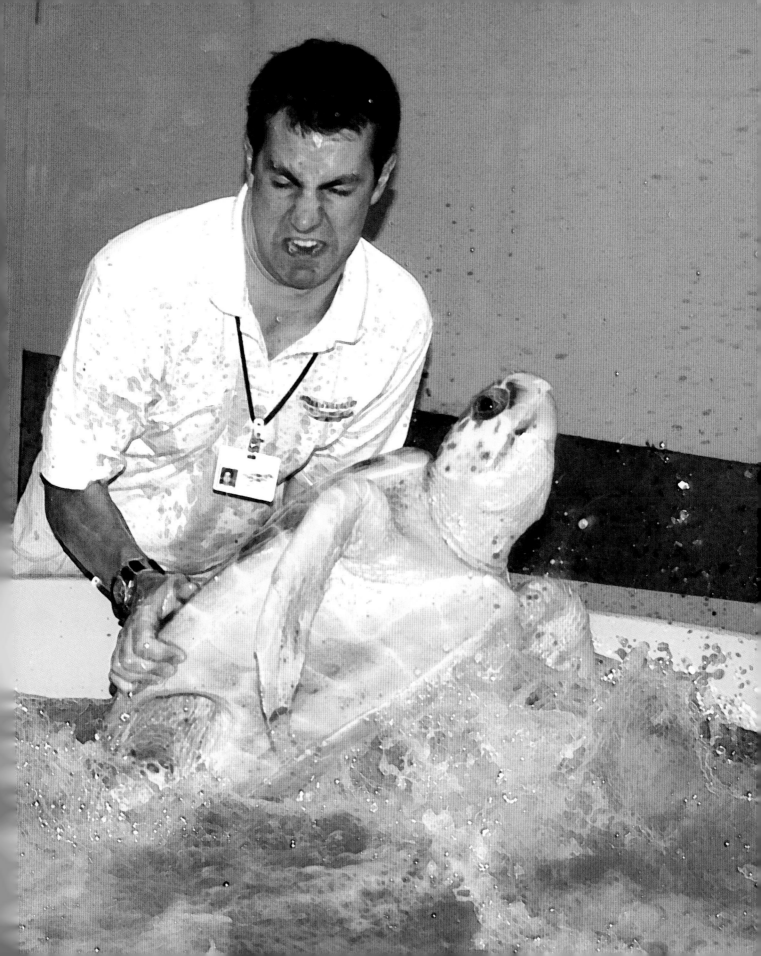

Carolina gained more and more
energy to play and explore her
new "home." She loved to play
with the water coming out of
the pipe into her tank.

Carolina loved watching all the people who worked at or visited the hospital. Sometimes she would swim over to say "Hi."

She liked watching the other turtles too. It made her feel better to know she was not alone in the hospital.

Finally, the big day was here. Carolina was going home! Everyone was excited for her, but they were sad to say "good-bye" to a friend. The staff and volunteers put Carolina in a truck and took her to a beach close to where she had been found four months earlier.

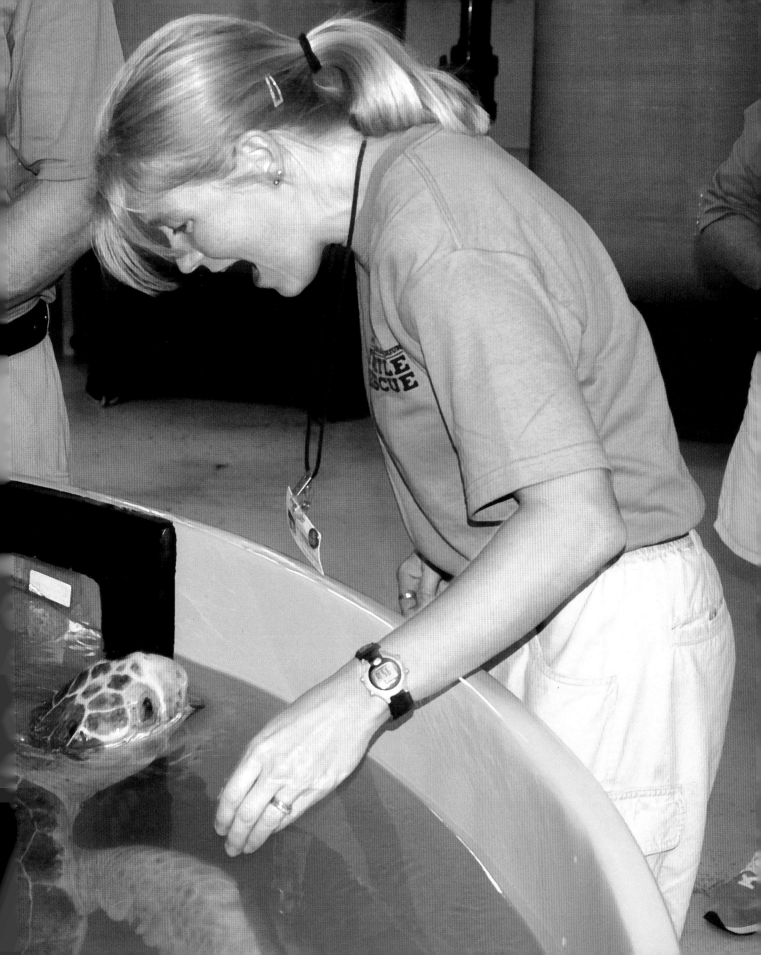

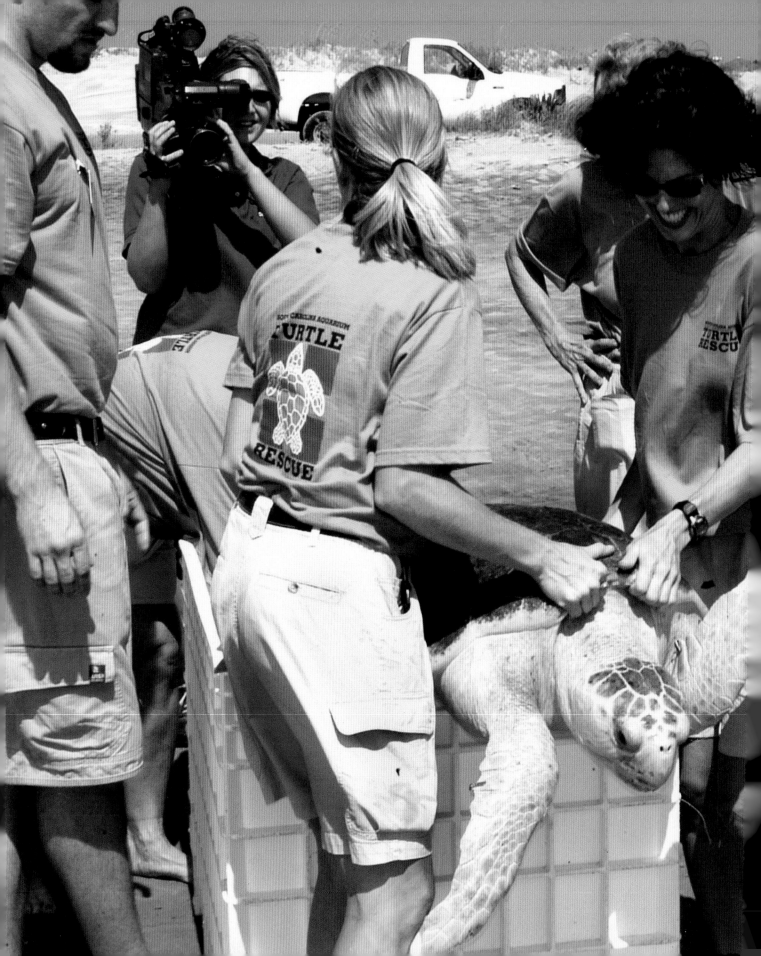

People carried
Carolina down
to the gently
lapping waves
and put her
down. At first
she didn't know
what to do. She
was scared and
confused.

When Carolina felt the water wash over her, her head came up in excitment as she recognized the ocean. She hurried as fast as she could. As she felt the sand disappear from beneath her, she was thankful to all the people who had helped her when she was sick. With one final look around, she headed to the deep ocean water... her home.

For Creative Minds - Turtle Fun Facts and Math Games

The top part of a turtle's shell is called a "carapace." The bottom part is called the "plastron." The shell is part of the turtle's body.

Sea turtles cannot pull their heads into their shells as can land turtles.

A female loggerhead sea turtle crawls onto the beach, digs a nest and lays 100 to 150 eggs. The eggs are about the size of a ping-pong ball and hatch after about two months.

The female loggerhead hatchlings that survive into adulthood will return to the same region to lay their eggs.

For the mom and the hatchlings, one way back to the ocean is to follow the reflected light of the moon or stars. During nesting season (May to October), keep outside beach lights turned off and pull down the shades at night to keep the light off the beach.

Turtles are reptiles. They are cold blooded and breathe air.

Because they breathe air, sea turtles must come to the surface of the ocean where they may be hit by boats.

Sea turtles, especially hatchlings, love to eat jellyfish (among other things) - because the jellyfish can't swim away!

Sea turtles often mistake floating plastic bags for jellyfish. The plastic can hurt the turtle (and other animals). Save a life, be sure to pick up the plastic bags!

Some sea turtles can hold their breath for up to four hours while they sleep. They like to hide in rocky areas to sleep.

A sea turtle needs sunlight to stay healthy - just like you!

A full grown loggerhead's shell is 3 to 3 1/2 feet in diameter. Measure the height of children to determine if they are smaller than, the same as, or larger in height than the diameter of a loggerhead's shell. By how much?

A full grown loggerhead sea turtle can weigh 360 pounds. If in a classroom, have students get into a group that totals about 360 pounds. If at home, figure out how much mom, dad, and children weigh. Add friends or grandparents as needed.

For sea turtle links, photos and updates on the turtles at the Sea Turtle Hospital, please go to SylvanDellPublishing.com and click on "Carolina's Story."

Make your own Sea Turtle

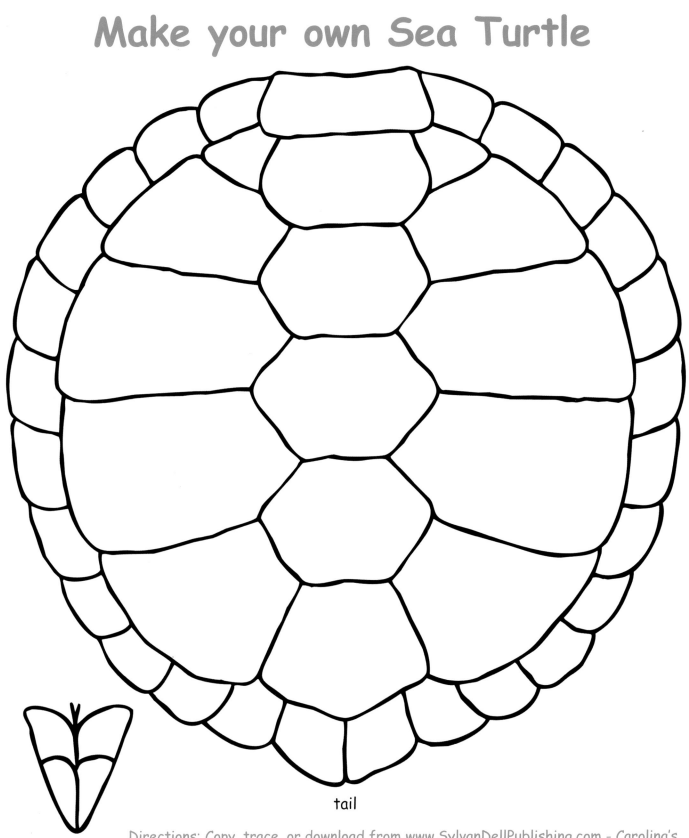

tail

Sea turtles have flippers to help them swim instead of claws or webbed feet with claws like other types of land or freshwater turtles.

left front flipper

right front flipper

A sea turtle's nose is cold - like a dog's!

rear flippers

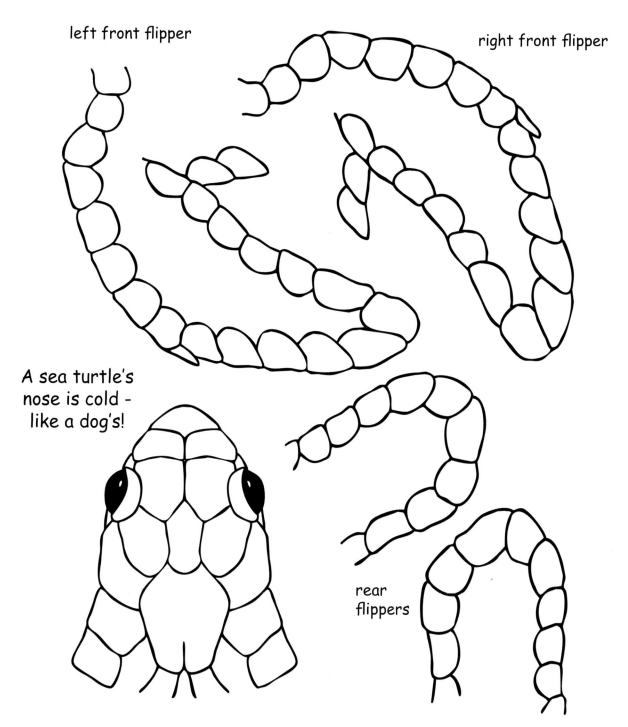

They use their front flippers for swimming and the back flippers for steering.

The sea-turtle craft illustrations are not scientifically accurate for a specific sea turtle.

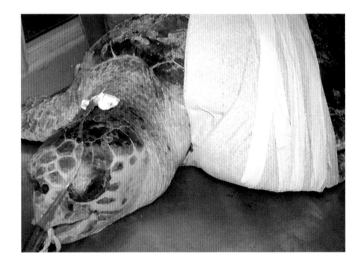

Hamlin (was trapped in a fishing pot line) after surgery with IV tubes. Dr. Tom tied down his flipper so he wouldn't rip out the stitches.

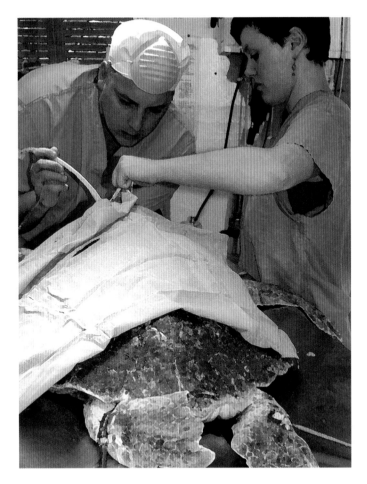

Channel (who was hit by a boat) has surgery.

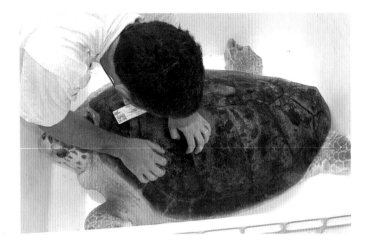

Big Girl (recovered from Turtle Flu) gets her back scratched just before her release.

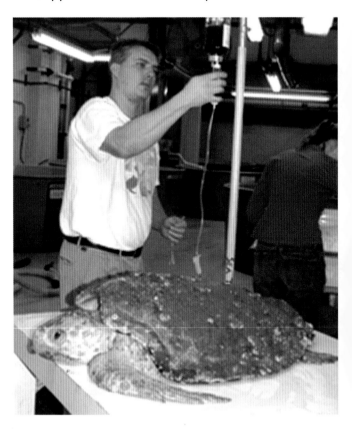

Litchfield (Turtle Flu) gets a blood transfusion with blood donated from another turtle.